WHAT ARE THE MEN WRITING IN THE SUGAR?

WHAT ARE THE MEN WRITING IN THE SUGAR?

Matty Bennett

QUEERMOJO
A Rebel Satori Imprint

New Orleans

Published in the United States of America by
REBEL SATORI PRESS
www.rebelsatori.com

Library of Congress Control Number: 2021931682

For Matteo

what distinguishes my face from a tree
is the total lack of commentary   as in that tree
loves you   honestly loves you   I'm the noisy one
who has to say it

—Heather Christle

WHAT ARE THE MEN WRITING IN THE SUGAR?

You say you like the cold, how it cracks
your hands and how that is a different kind
        of cracked from home. It's warm in Sicily.
Dry, searing summers on the sea. *Io mangio*
        la mela. I no longer have to imagine
how lovely you are, sweating in the sand,
        underneath a flowery umbrella, blue and
orange, leaning back on your elbows, dark
        brown moles accentuated on your protected
pale skin. *Tu leggi il giornale.* Most days I walk
        down the sweaty asphalt road to work, pass
the same people, the same trees, the same
        lady in the same Accord at the same time each
week day. When we kissed for the first time
        on the asphalt outside my apartment, my lungs
roared like hot air balloons. *Gli uomini scrivono*
        nello zucchero. On that second date I finished
your beer and you asked me how to live
        in a poem. We had a lot of trouble deciding
where to sit in the restaurant. There was music
        we liked, and the bass vibrated our chests.
You leaned in close, spoke up so I could hear.

NPR SAYS THIS IS CUFFING SEASON

Sheets of ice, everywhere. Or, maybe,
future ocean waves lapping against our feet.

Winter, even at its cruelest, brings contingence,
and, gratefully, my affinity for you. In retrospect,

I'm glad I spent three years playing pool in bars
instead of writing poems. The ice, it's fine.

My shoes have no traction. I will pull you down
with me, beams of headlights merging,

edifying us in the street. Yes, I'll admit, I am
artless, a clodhopper, if you will—touch me

anywhere. There is so much I need to tell you,
like how my hands, cracked and cold, smoldered

when I shut your car door, when I walked up
my east side steps, alone, when I scrolled

through hundreds of men, solitary, still, and, also,
how you are, all at once, everything I want

and completely unknown to me. I want to put
my bare hands on the ice, speed up this process.

Side-step. Oncoming traffic. Your steady hand, slowly dismantling a giant Jenga tower, and then, relief.

10-DAY FORECAST

I've lost those Saturdays
of crashing. I used to be
an architect of clouds, purple
and thick, bursting showers
of lavender over the town,
violent, loud, never-ending
until the streets turned empty.
I used to lie there, arms spread
across lanes looking up
toward nothing, the blueprints
forever the same: place the clouds
in their heads, puncture them
with scissors, slice
until the lavender fills their bodies.
6 years later I step
onto your mother's terrace
in Ragusa, Sicily. A garden
of organized green chaos.
Dry heat. I hear you and your mother
speaking in Italian, I hear an outline
of the day: the sea, *granita*,
sitting on beach towels
so salt won't seep into the seats
of your Volkswagen Lupo,
In Alto Mare in the car, windows down,
your hand on my thigh
even through the *tornante* turns,
that which comes back, no words.

When we get to the sea,
you tell me the yellow flags
at the lifeguard stand mean
caution. The sea feels cold
sliding past our shins,
and I crane my neck back
to see the sky sear blue.

A DICEMBRE RITORNI IN ITALIA
IN DECEMBER YOU RETURN TO ITALY

It took you years
to debut your face
to the social
media masses.
You started
with Christmas
lights and a risk
of death.
It's no surprise
I'm shadows
and fragments.
You teach me
Sicilian card games
your family plays
at Christmas:
scopa, briscola.
Eventually you
moved on
to two black cats
in the sink.
Their camera
green eyes told you:
*mind your own
business.*
Bicontinental.
I praise the vast

distance and gift it
everything I have:
the millions of
seconds when
both feet were
off the ground
as I ran. *If you
can't already tell,
this game is
mostly luck.*

FIRST DATE

Once I thought I would write
a poem after every date I had
with a man named Jack,
and I would present him the poems
on our wedding night: Poem #3
was titled "BREAKUP." This is something
I don't mention. Another is that
I climb trees when I'm just drunk
enough with confidence, my arms
a little stronger, looser, free.
I think 5:00 p.m. is late
for coffee. You say a relationship
is like a project. In 6th grade
Hillary Brown and I flipped coins
to assign our baby various genes.
He had a cleft chin. I dive into
your brown eyes, our mugs
of coffee reflect February gray.
There's a lot I don't understand
about the economy. Later I wander
around Broadway, listen to Four Tet,
a record called *New Energy*
you share with me: a soundtrack
for my feet against the asphalt.

FOR NOW, GOOD NIGHT

> "If I open the door he'll flash and fade
> like heat lightning behind a bank of clouds
> one summer night at the edge of the world."
> —Mark Bibbins

All the men finally died, and that
was a wonderful thing. I knew
exactly where it would happen:
the beds they never slept in. Their legs
gliding like gazelles, their arms
by their sides, then on their knees.
They were all equestrian-themed,
unicorn stamps on their hands
that never washed off, and too much
tequila. All the men said their love
swelled, in piles of wolf pictures
never hung, and they waited
for more secrets. They imagined
themselves as hidden artifacts,
either sacred or tired of humanity.
When they died, thousands of purple
flower buds opened at the base
of a mountain and said *thank you.*

ALL MY BREAKUPS WERE HALLOWEEN

The ending is obvious: no one's screaming
when his eyes are darts, the bystander effect.

He wears a large white sheet over his body,
three black holes. I didn't realize I was holding

my hands out like a beggar. People gift me
solemn sighs, the distracted ones candy.

I'll clasp their pity in a locket and bury it
in some unmarked grave for a sequel.

I could object, make a scene: I don't. Post
severance, I lie on a bed of leaves, arms

stiff as witches brooms, and the spiders
befriend me. Up close they are fuzzy,

eight black opal eyes that reflect crystals
and innocence. They say we'll hunt together

in the dimness of dusk and moonlight.
There are three things I will try to remember

about today: the moment he finally floats
away, disappearing into the dark forest

as he gobbles more men with his gaping
mouth hole, how wolf spider eyes shine

brightly in torchlight, and, after he vanished,

how I sprung open like a vampire's cape.

MATTEO, MATTEO

One time was never enough,
on the asphalt outside the hot pot,
I refused to let that kiss be
the last. You are more rocketship
than anything I ever have conceived:
peach fuzz, the whole world here
in your spider fingertips, a disco ball
above our grooving heads.
At the Parcels concert in Boston,
the sparkly silver curtain reflects
rainbows, me in a denim jacket
you say you can't pull off,
and thoughts of what it was like
to be gay in the '80s. Now every halo
of light holds your image: the tiny elevator
in our hotel in Rome that will barely fit
you and your turquoise luggage, I'll take
the stairs and watch your ascent.
We will shower together in Montreal,
you will lather your hands into my skull
for what feels like clouds. The two of us
huddled underneath a red Iberia blanket,
hovering somewhere over the Atlantic.

USAGE OF THE WORD SOBER
HAS STEADILY DECLINED SINCE 1800

This time, I am a man whose sheets
are crisp in the morning. In the fireglow,
I do not force my mind to form
your shadow on the walls of my bedroom,
animal spirit cards strewn about the carpet.
Just a sip of wine. Sometimes the curtains
move a bit, even when there is no draft,
and you say *ghosts*. It's snowing
again, and there may be a worthwhile
temperance in this, but for tonight,
I give into your Bleu de Chanel, press
my face into your concave chest, lift
your arms like the leaves of an orchid
firmly rooted in bark, so as to remove
every layer of clothing. There's soft
white snow behind the shades,
and the lamplight fuses our contours
into one, and we spin through wild breaths,
and I slide my tongue up your ribs,
your skin a relentless showcase.

TIME-DELAY FUSE

My loneliness was like the day after the Fourth of July—fireworks
seventy percent off, then stuffed in the back of a broom closet.
Another year would expire, fit into a passing *hello, good morning*.
My passion was a dusty box of sparklers paid for and forgotten.
My chest was indulgent, not perfect. For years I thought, alone in
bed, another head would mold to me nicely. The first Fourth of July
we spent together was down by the Providence Harbor: crowds of
bustling families, children on their neon scooters, panting dogs in
the thick summer air. The boats sent flames into the hazy sky, and
the greens and purples blurred in the calm waves. Our hands burst
into peony shells, clasped together as the colors tumbled toward
the water. In the dark of your room, we lay on our backs, naked,
and my ribs bloomed beneath my skin: bones of orange and yellow
cascaded through our night like a glitter willow.

INSTAGRAM STORYBURST
JULY 2019

*

You tell the world, worry not:
the drop of SP68 Rosso 2016
that looks like blood
is excellent.

*

We're speeding through
the Sicilian countryside in your
Lupo, and the dust billows
into the xeric landscape
peppered with cork oaks.
You are always late.

*

I help you button up your flowery green
collared shirt as we stride over to the group.
The Norwegians on the wine tour are

DJs: *dance with us.* Sweat slides down
our necks under vineyard sun, *a vintage
that will behave well over time.*

*

I wish Duolingo had
an Italian lesson on what to say
when meeting your boyfriend's parents
for the first time.

*

A New York City mom
shares with the world that her little baby girl
smiles at everyone: no prejudice. These smiles
have lifted her out of a depression.

*

When I painted *everyone
smiles in the same language*
on an elementary school mural, you said
you've never had the desire to hang
a painting outside your window

for the town to see.

*

Dov'è l'uva? Where are the grapes?
It isn't time. We go underground
to see huge concrete containers stained
in light red, ready to be filled.

*

Dov'è Arianna?
The woman with the wine
who's conquering the world,
a hundred thousand bottles
last year. Some showed up
in Rhode Island, but you said we should wait
until Italy. *It tastes like
the land it was born from.*

*

You have all these
photographs of me, reaching for
an almond hanging from a tree,

17

our naked reflections in the TV screen,
and no one will ever see.

DISPLAY OF AFFECTION

In the beginning, you didn't understand
how anyone could have so much morning
energy. We have woken up 10,000 times.
I have inspected your neck just a few hundred,
enough to see your skin rising and falling
like a little trampoline. A TED Talk attempts
to quantify love with science, spends most
of the speech quoting famous poets. *It felt
like jumping in the sky.* This journal needs
to contain almost everything, like skin:
then you take a sip in soft yellow, then my
relentless need to describe the rings
of espresso that remain when you leave.

MAYBE I'M NOT IN LOVE

quite yet, but I said the words,
on your bed, a little drunk,
the thunderstorm flashed

so quickly as we stood in line
for the spring concert, Yaeji,
rain, make it rain, girl, make it,

and we ran to your apartment,
ripped off our wet clothes,
spontaneous sex, light

flickers, doors wide open. Earlier
in the booth of the grad center bar,
I attempted to show your friends

how much Italian I'd learned
in just a few months (*No,
non ho un cane o un gatto!*).

I said the words and you wrote
them off, this new language
a portal. You went to get me

some water, so I gave myself
a pep talk: *sono un'anatra,
I am a duck,* thought maybe

my arms would flap a brilliant
green and somehow I would
glide across water, but *I love you*

traveled like a frisbee crashing
into every tree. Then, when you
returned: *sono una volpe, I am*

a fox, I will destroy the ducks,
le anatre, I will end their relentless
quacking, I will demolish every

flap and ripple they create. I was
una volpe, but still just a man
in love, sprinting around, trying

to bury his head into the ground.

THE ONES THAT KEEP US

For every three breaths you take

in Missouri, you take just one

in Rhode Island. It's the heat,

the humidity, science. Maybe

it's too much family, too much

Midwest. The moment before
goodbye, vacation ending, you

went for the handshake, Dad

went for the hug: hummingbird

over both your shoulders,

rocking quick and content

on his little swing, the summer

forest swelling toward the house.

All the stock photos of *trust*

include someone extending

a hand over some crevice

or cliff to another human.
The Missouri River bluffs we

climbed, another expansive view,

a photo to add to next year's

anniversary flip book. Maybe

this year we could fill the book

with the reasons behind every sigh:

12-13 an hour. Let's limit them

to the ones that keep us

from dying: I drove you

to the airport, you buried your face

into my forearm, the tennis court
of my lungs desperate to unfold.

18 EUROS LEFT IN MY WALLET

That summer we jumped
into a painting of red foxes.
Arid mountains behind us,
the Mediterranean Sea before.

Beach towel capes, fists
in the air. Under water, you
grabbed hold of me, nothing
could stop my throbbing.

I learned a lot that summer:
how to be a corpse

in the sea, how to keep
a door propped. The train

station. I couldn't breathe.

I never heard *I love you.*

IF YOU WROTE ME A POEM

it would be a math equation.
It would be methodical. It would
not mention love, how it is pink

sunlight or how it is a baby
duck's orange feet flailing
underwater as he learns to swim.

It would be straightforward.
We sat at the kitchen table. We
drank espresso. We listened to NPR.

There would be no commentary,
no exclamations or proclamations.
No—*espresso! You grip me*

with your robust, dark hand,
fling me toward the sky, give me
life!—even if you are thinking this.

Even if you could not imagine
a day without a warm buzz.
Your poem is what we

could prove together:
Is love enough
of a reason to get married?

Your answer is no, the subsequent
stanzas would list all the reasons
why. Solutions themselves

often hold more interesting questions:
*How can we feel safe in love? How
can you ever really trust someone?*

*I water the plants. I think of past loves
and feel simultaneously grateful,
damaged. I do not feel like*

*a Chinese Money plant, no. I do not
feel like a housewarming gift
or sign of prosperity. Instead, I am*

*the Devil's Ivy. Leave me in
darkness, neglect to water me,
and I continue to shine green.*

WE CAN TOPPLE THEM OVER IF YOU'D LIKE

You hand me   an espresso
        I don't ask for: your head
                is a room I wish to rent.

                We've traipsed all over Sicily

        searching for espresso cups,
        the rainbow ones, *colorati,*

        just like your mom has
                in the cupboard where,
with just one wrong move,
                everything crashes.

    In the terrace garden
        I marvel at the number
                of plastic bags your mom has
                hanging from door knobs,
        off the backs of chairs,
each containing little mysteries
        (*How long has this bag*
of apricot pits been here?).

        Maybe Modica will have
                the cups we want. Maybe
        they're in the bell tower.

Maybe every option today

is a kind of falling. Walking

through the streets of Pozzallo,
pastel laundry ripples over

our heads.

I don't ever have to knock on your door.

Back home, I order the cups
online, stack them neatly
on the kitchen counter.

Each morning, you hand me
mismatched cups and saucers.
Yellow and blue, white and orange.

Sometimes when we embrace,
you make your body limp, sliding

slowly to the ground, and I use

all my strength to hold you up.

INSTAGRAM STORYBURST
OCTOBER 2019

*

This baby receptionist refused
to be photographed to protect his job,
but he told you about the long
working hours and, among other things,
the lack of milk in the vending machines.
This must be stopped, you tell the world.
Everyone nods their heads.

*

Also the spiders. You ask me
if I can hear them singing,
and when I get out of bed,
you tell me they have wrapped
their webs around my ankles
like shackles. The silence of the woods
breaks when the coyotes start laughing.

*

All the other trees of autumn
are dead, except for the one shining
like a yellow diamond above the rest.

*

Your extended family thinks
I'm just *un amico, a friend,*
the smiling, nodding American.

*

A stranger
standing in front of you wears
a pink bomber jacket, the words
BE POLIT embroidered on the back.
You tell the world: *you better be polit*
with me stranger, or may you die
strangled by rose branches
and stung by a thousand wasps.

*

Someone says: *you have*
quite the imagination. The turkey
in the crosswalk is technically not
a pedestrian, but you've caught it
and kept it in your apartment
for a week so: *let's eat.*

*

When Zio Peppino gets up to leave,
he smiles through missing teeth
and asks me *in italiano*
what my tattoos mean,
and you quickly usher him out the door.

*

A flurry of parking garage images,
often architectural afterthought,
a stunning facade lit with an offset array
of colored light in blue, green, and red.
Its heartbeat pulses
with the vibrancy of the city.

*

I lean over the edge,
back shiny, hot tub froth,
hair slicked, snow on the trees.
This, you decided, something
for the world to see.

[WE'RE AT THE POINT WHERE] PEOPLE ARE DEFINING ME IN TERMS OF YOU

Thirst can be champagne
fountains, mostly when the men
have had their fill. Their eyes,
I used to let them sift through
ribbon fingers. *Gay men never
stay with their first love,
honey.* Here is a room filled
with arcade games. I am laser-
focused on *Killer Instinct*:
I'm Orchid, the only female
fighter, a scantily clad gymnast
who morphs into an acrobatic
tiger. A wink from a man wearing
a Mario crop top; we went
on one date. I don't want any
of this back. It will always
be here. And the disco lights
spinning on the platform
glitter like a Las Vegas stage.
I'm up there. I'm Britney. I'm
floating above the crowd: a sparkly
skin-baring angel in a ring of fire,
the pageantry darkly pounding
where every night is opening night.

IMPRESSION, VISIBILITY

I was twenty on a Thursday night,
and I owned a heritage I knew nothing
about: pink neon wristbands, dolled-up
drag queens, and the thumpa-thumpa

pulsing through the sticky floors.
From the back room, I saw flashing
strobe lights and thick clouds
of cigarette smoke. I had black X's

on my hands. At the urinal, an old man
craned his neck to stare at my cock.
I wished I was drunk. The night groaned.
Shirts came off and smooth chests gyrated.

I heard *nice outfit* as if I wore a costume:
plaid button-down, old jeans, ratty
brown boots. I walked home, and snow
fell in the orange glow of street lamps.

There was no warm breath on my neck. I am
a lineage of men born on the Mississippi,
gutting deer and mounting antlers
on the wall. I am the blood of leathery men

working in wheat fields, an entire life spent
under the blistering sun. I am men buying
pheasants, spinning them around just to

shoot them down. I am a photograph

of Grandpa in the bunker during the Korean War.
He's doing a handstand, back muscles
glistening in the hot sun. I am the photograph
where he's holding a gun, staring intently

at the camera. I thought leaving would
somehow make me feel seen. I thought
I would feel at home. I thought there would be
someone in bed next to me in the morning.

HANGOVER CURE

I'm finally starting to forget
the wasted breaths. I can't keep
track of each inhale that led me
toward humanness. My cure
for a day was pressing my palms
to scalding coffee mugs.
The worst part: not being able to
practice my hair flip in the shower
because I'd make myself puke, or
the coffee pot's final steam sigh
at the sight of my trembling hands.
I found a few cures: when the wind
became my long hair, when the leaves
trailed across the asphalt behind me
like a billowy wedding gown train,
and then, after you, when I stretched
out my arms and spun in circles
forming rings of trees in my room.

THE TAMARACK TREES

"Over the weekend
we could turn the world to gold."
—Carly Rae Jepsen

I used to dream of flying
into white peaks, tamaracks

bursting yellow under little
hats of snow, but you are

everywhere, all at once
like black sky. This is new.

I don't need you to tell me
the trees are still golden:

your teeth are my nightlight.
Stars beneath peacoats.

When I described a flower
arrangement as lovely

I was told *men don't say
lovely.* Autumn's caress

is my jaw against
your ribs, the creak

of the tamarack tree
like a door opening.

NOTHING HAPPENS OVERNIGHT

Hans on the refrigerator in red letters
like a horror film: HANS WAS HERE.
Hans was with Michael for eight years,

married for two, and then one day
woke up and said: *I don't love you
anymore.* Michael, shattered, shaved

his head like Britney, posted pictures
all over the Internet of the new life
he had to create. Who's to say it's right

or wrong to go through breakups publicly,
posting every emotion, dyed hair, new
tattoo. We're millennials: this is our right.

We are standing in your family
summer *appartamento* on the sea
in Pozzallo. No one's been here

for a couple summers. It's dusty,
hot, and full of *insetti* in the bathtub.
The sex we have days into the trip is

urgent, in front of the fan, elbows
on the kitchen table, a flit of my hand
across your face, ends abruptly:

we can't leave a trace. I ask my therapist,
what if one day, one of us wakes up
and says I don't love you anymore?

She says: *No one can break*
a relationship if there isn't already
a crack. Nothing happens overnight.

The next morning, I write my name
on the fridge with the red dry erase maker:
MATTY THE AMERICAN WAS HERE.

THE TUMBLEWEEDS

I hadn't yet touched
your hands.

Mine were
tumbleweeds.

I wanted a dog,
but he was

a tumbleweed.
My feet were

tumbleweeds,
the world spinning

in the most colorless
way. Some nights

I looked into
a kaleidoscope:

there was turquoise,
then there were

more tumbleweeds.
Still. I hope you

never know me

as the beige

of my bedroom walls,
my comforter,

the color that woke me
every morning.

I liked it when
you took my hands,

transformed me
into a snowman,

and draped a rainbow
around my neck.

Though I did learn a lot
from the asphalt:

how to runway
walk, vodka soda

in hand, how
to see through

sequins, how
to be a complete

disaster. Some
people repurpose

tumbleweeds
into centerpieces.

CUTE BOY ENERGY

1

In the movie *Ever After*, Leonardo Di Vinci places
Cinderella's glass slipper on a castle ledge. He sets
it down so matter-of-factly, like how I set down the rolls
on the Thanksgiving table when neither of us brought
the vegetable dish. Prince Charming yells: *I will not yield!*

2

A potted Devil's Ivy you gave me last summer,
branches spiraling toward the floor. I always lose
to you at Monopoly, and although I have a leg up
in Bananagrams, I don't always win. "Alarmingly," they say,
the process of balance deterioration starts at age 25.

3

When I was 8, playing in the storage room of my childhood
home, there were passionate invisible men. It was exhausting
keeping up with them, running through the concrete room,
twirling around wooden posts. I would grab them by the neck,
pull them close to my face and blow them a soft kiss.

4

Late night in my dark living room, we slow dance
as Taylor Swift drifts around us: *don't read
the last page*. You used to hate her, now you merely
dislike her. Your black shoes next to my front door,
they create little puddles from the snow.

5

The morning after, I took a photograph of your
contacts case on the edge of my bathroom sink
because it was a historic moment. You take so long
getting ready for bed: whether early or late we still
exit the world together, warm the sheets with our skin.

SAI COME SONO I RAGAZZI
YOU KNOW HOW BOYS ARE

You ask: is there anything hotter
than this perfect drop of plant fluid

on the tip of the new leaf
of my spider plant?

Red lip stains. Jean jacket.
80's blue and pink decor

of the Laundry Club.
Self-portrait on your Rothko.

Your shirtless reflection,
messy hair, glasses, slender

black mustache I gently slide
my index finger across. That time

you were too tired to have sex,
so I suggested we talk about

our feelings. *I take it back, let's
just have sex.* Everyone can see you

in this museum. I can only be
seen in the broken mirror,

our heads distorted, fractured.
I float over your shoulder.

One of the first things I learned
on Italian Duolingo: *sai come sono*

i ragazzi, you know how boys are.

Boys like the words *open relationship.*

You wrung your hands over and over,

silent on my navy blue couch,

my head in your chest. I was nauseous

at dinner that night, not just because

of the fried chicken. Boy, if I could just

squeeze your shoulder a little

harder. If I could just press
our foreheads together,

create a diamond sparkling
like Christmas lights in fresh snow.

Boys and their blueprints
for the future, some say a fool's

errand, and yet: we speak
of Seattle, of Sweden, of a little girl

named Chiara, of weddings
in Ragusa. After a month

with the Atlantic between
us, I wait with a glittery welcome

home sign above my head: a boy
in a cat sweatshirt in desperate need

of a haircut, a boy who thinks
he's got everything figured out.

TEAM HUDDLE

We are wrapped up: autumnal air
spirals pollen through my open

nighttime window, and the crisp
world hovers, our silhouettes

buried beneath my grandma's quilt.
Your warm breath on my neck

folds lyrics into my skin. In the car
that night you sang *tell me all*

the ways to love you into your fist,
a little boy's grin. The orchid

you gave me on Valentine's Day.
It doesn't need much light to grow,

and I don't need much
except the slide of your hand

around my belly at 3 a.m.
If I could no longer see you

crawling out of our bed
in the navy blue morning,

white briefs and white socks,

would you breathe outlines

of all the objects we need
to get through the cold, the dying?

My piano, your gold glasses, a cat?
Take me with you through the house,

and put your hands on my hands
for the smallest of tasks.

DID YOU MAKE ANY DREAMS LAST NIGHT?

You're walking home now, sliding across
the icy sidewalks, everything glittery
and blazing: the morning sun is a giant
present with a big red bow. Funeral notices
hanging on stone walls around town.
They said the spirit of your Grandpa
still grinds his teeth beyond the grave,
and as you walk away, I see a hawk perched
on the powerline. So still, so much to do.
I can see the orange *don't walk* sign flashing
a couple blocks away. You always say
you *made a dream* instead of *had*, and this
makes me feel as though I have control
over what I dream, like how with each sunset
I can find a new hue, some large brushstroke,
loud and bright, or subdued and stained,
name it, identify it, describe it incessantly until
it becomes my own. I put everything on display
these days: bouquet of white roses exploding
from my mouth, hands scribbling as many
love notes as they can, magnetic letters
on the fridge, hoping someday they'll say we
were more than the sound of grinding teeth.

IN THE FAR, FAR FUTURE

If my memories appeared
outside my head, they would look

like a string of cut-out
construction paper people,

never-ending, accordion-style,
array of colors, classic ones

from the bulk package: reds,
greens, blues, but also

the white sheets that are really
just computer paper. Some

of the cut-out people would have
long, long legs, spiraling all around

like an orchid's aerial roots.
We could plant the little people

next fall and raise them in the spring
as our giant family, however,

the adamant Aussie man giving
his speech about successful couples

says: the best thing to do to save

your future marriage is to first

get older. This requires sunsets.
I'd like to order one over every

body of water. I'd like to add
whales as well, the ones that hold

their breath for 2 hours,
so that when they burst through

the surface, we capture them
at the exact moment the air

fulfills their lungs, and their entire
bodies smile. Also add a tiny iceberg

to the left. I know pacing
concerns you, so I will write *time*

inside a construction paper card
and gift it to you at Christmas,

but this requires another year.
By then I'll want to throw *time*

into the fireplace, which isn't
functional, the crackling yule log

comes from YouTube, so I will
chuck *time* into the television screen,

watch it bounce off the glass, smash it
into my winter boots, take your hand

and go for a walk through the snow.
I think it's starting to flurry.

ARIA, ADAGIO

While you sleep, my fingers press fortunes
into your skin, and I create purple universes
in each touch, ones with tiny dragons
that have big, round eyes, and I try to think

of the millions of little decisions that formed
your slight frame, how when we wake
you hover above me like a gentle astronaut,
your signature sigh, how I know for those

few seconds I have so much power.
There's a book of which I refuse to read
the last few pages, lingering, absolutely certain
of how something will explode, then,

over thousands of years, float toward
something perfect, and, also, how I know
almost nothing, desperate for answers, like how
I always know where your glasses are.

The lights on the airport roof are a beacon,
a young boy spinning around shining his teeth.
There were those stupid nights passed out
on the floor of my apartment on Westcott.

I almost froze to death on the steps, I rang
the doorbell dozens of times at 4 in the morning
in the snow. I don't remember being let inside.

I had no idea and yet I was certain, fists clenched

to your existence. Years later you climbed out
of your white '98 Corolla, crossed Broadway
and we headed into Seven Stars Bakery
together, a Sunday evening, a handwritten note

on my calendar. There were other things listed,
too: write poems, go for a run, practice piano,
be a man in love and let that be everything,
water the plants, Matty, and speak kindly

to them. Someday, you'll have brown spots
on your hands just like the crispy fern. Someday,
every morning will be espresso e panettone,
my fingertips playing Bach on your forearm.

WHY YOU REFUSE TO WATCH CALL ME BY YOUR NAME

I've been a pair of sunglasses, the kind they pass out
for free on the quad, meant for an outdoor spring concert,
a slew of indie-electronic bands with no hits.

I've been the pair resting on the bridge
of Timothee Chalamet's nose, the scene in the pool
where he's pretending to work on his music. *Thinking, then.*

I've been the pair you can't find, I've been the pair you
weren't sure you should buy, the shop in Montreal, *English*
or French? Yes, I was that yellow pair, you bought the brown.

Those aren't sunglasses, those are two brick buildings
painted black. Your straight friends say: *ok, so,*
it's about two men in love? This is no longer ground-breaking.

I've been the pair you wear when the Italian sun is setting
and you're not ready to let the day go. Now we're sitting
on your couch, and it's time to decide, decide, decide.

All this dancing business in the discotheque would be
easier with sunglasses, so I close my eyes, emulate
Timothee Chalamet dancing to "Love My Way."

I want us to take off our sunglasses, jump inside Elio's dream
his last night with Oliver. That day, they escaped into

the wilderness, let out primal screams of each other's names,

could finally tousle each other's hair. In his dreamscape: flashes
of their warm red bodies, falling over each other to reach
the crashing waterfall, isolated, together, and absolutely free.

BIG ENOUGH FOR US

I will never leave a dense fog behind. I am
an open umbrella for us: when our eyes lock,
when our hands are greasy. I will have too many
words for you: when we slept in the tiny cabin
on the lake in New Hampshire, we heard *le anatre,*
the ducks, loud, louder, their quacking creeping
closer, surrounding us, enclosing us, then:
chatter, grunt, groan, *sigh*. When you gave me
the wooden duck that now sits above our fireplace,
when you pulled a Calluna heather plant from
your backpack for me, when you led me through
the village of Ragusa Ibla and we rounded cobblestone
corners, snuck kisses, hiding from the orange warmth
of street lamps, and when you touched my hand
in front of your parents in their terrace garden,
a little green corner opened for us to exist.

WHAT WILL WE WRITE IN THE SUGAR?

My first instinct is to write
my name in cursive and draw

a heart: how can you change
an instinct? I'm waiting

for the cheerfulness
paperwhites you gave me

to bloom before I leave
for Christmas, otherwise

what's the point?
The instructions are to turn

the vase one quarter each day
to avoid leaning. We missed

most of the sun today,
dancing to reggaeton

past 3 a.m., folding our bodies
into one another all night.

My next instinct
is to write your name

just to see what it looks like

next to mine.

The *and* is necessary.
Unlike the sand, our names

stay as long as we'd like,
no sea to wash us away.

Yesterday, I forgot to turn
the flowers: it's impossible

to keep from leaning
toward the things we love,

what we crash through
windows for, what we blossom

again from the gutter for,
what we stare into the sun for.

I will keep writing just to see
the letters, just to see.

NOTES

The title of this collection is inspired by an introductory Italian Duolingo lesson in which you are taught the phrase *gli uomini scrivono nello zucchero*, meaning *the men write in the sugar.*

The epigraph for this collection is taken from Heather Christle's poem titled "Trying to Return the Sun" from her poetry collection *The Trees The Trees.*

"10-Day Forecast" references the song "In Alto Mare" by Loredana Bertè.

"For Now, Good Night" has an epigraph from a Mark Bibbins poem titled "And You Thought You Were the Only One" from his collection *Sky Lounge.*

"Instagram Storyburst July 2019" references language from the website for the Occhipinti winery in Ragusa, Sicily.

"Display of Affection" references a TED talk titled *The brain in love* by Helen Fisher.

"Maybe I'm Not In Love" includes lyrics from the song "raingurl" by Yaeji.

"The Tamarack Trees" has an epigraph from a Carly Rae Jepsen song titled "Runaway With Me."

"Cute Boy Energy" includes lyrics from the song "New Year's Day" by Taylor Swift.

"Team Huddle" includes lyrics from the song "Lucky Strike" by Troye Sivan.

"In The Far, Far Future" references a TED talk titled 3 *ways to build a happy marriage and avoid divorce* by George Blair-West.

"Why You Refuse to Watch Call Me By Your Name" references the song "Love My Way" by The Psychedelic Furs.

ACKNOWLEDGMENTS

First and foremost, thank you for reading this collection of poems. When I set out to write this book, my goal was to create a celebration of gay male love. Thank you for supporting a gay author, a queer-owned press, and for celebrating love with me.

Thank you to my poetic partner in creativity Lisa Summe. I deeply value our friendship, and your guidance throughout this process has been vital. Your time and energy in helping me craft these poems is sincerely appreciated.

Thank you to my colleague and mentor Jeff Mann for your generous help with the editing of these poems and for believing this book was worthy of publication.

Thank you to my thesis advisor Erika Meitner for pushing me to be a critical reader of my own work. This book could not have been made without your guidance during my MFA at Virginia Tech and beyond. You taught me to be my own best editor, and for that I am eternally grateful.

Thank you to Phim Her, Sarah Anthony, Rukayat Oloko, and Luisa Ardila for your creative community, constant support, and your encouragement of my work over the years. What started as a senior poetry class at Syracuse University has turned into lasting friendships and a forever workshop that I continue to cherish.

Thank you to the editors of *Juked, Homology Lit, Cardiff Review, Lammergeier Magazine, Watershed Review, The Bookends Review,*

Philadelphia Gay News, *IO Lit*, and the *Queerbook Anthology* at Giovanni's Room for publishing many of these poems, or earlier versions of them.

Thank you to Mark Bibbins and Alex Dimitrov for taking the time to write such generous blurbs about this collection. You are two of my biggest role models and inspirations. Your time and thoughtfulness is sincerely appreciated.

Thank you to Sirin Thada for illustrating the cover for this collection. Working with you was such a joy, and you captured the spirit of the collection wonderfully.

Thank you to my publisher Sven of Rebel Satori Press for your kindness, enthusiasm for my work, and for giving my debut collection of poetry a home.

E, infine, al mio ragazzo Matteo Iudice, grazie di tutto.

CPSIA information can be obtained
at www.ICGtesting.com
Printed in the USA
BVHW031548220421
605634BV00004B/430

9 781608 641550